CHARMING
Charli CEO

ISBN 9781562295233

Christian Living Books, Inc.
P.O. Box 7584
Largo, MD 20792
christianlivingbooks.com
We bring your dreams to fruition.

Charli Southall & DeAnna Lewis

Illustrated by Darrien Lindsey

CHRISTIAN LIVING
B O O K S

Largo, MD

In a world full of lemon trees, out of a need, I started my own lemonade business. Yes, lil ole me, Charli without the E. I'm gonna share with you how my business came to be.

On a beautiful Saturday afternoon, Charli was out playing happily in her backyard. Suddenly, something happened. Charli became very thirsty. She wanted some ice-cold, yummy juice to quench her thirst.

Charli rushed into the house, opened her refrigerator, and looked for something to drink. But all she saw was a bottle of plain water. Charli didn't want water. She wanted a cool, refreshing, and sweet drink.

She shut the fridge door in disappointment and searched all the cabinets hoping to find just one box of juice—but she found nothing, nada, zilch.

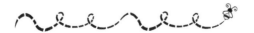

C harli looked out her kitchen window. Right there in her very own backyard was a lemon tree full of juicy, yellow lemons. And out of the blue, she had a big idea.

S he rushed back outside
and said, "I will make
my own cool, refreshing,
and sweet drink."

Charli gathered all the lemons she could carry in her hands and hurried back inside. Then she stopped: "Wait!" she said. "I don't know how to make lemonade."

She grabbed her iPad and asked Google the important question, "How do you make lemonade from lemons?"

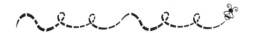

Charli washed all the lemons and rolled them on the kitchen counter to make them soft and squeezable. Then she asked her mom to help her cut them in half. She and her mom squeezed all the juice out of the lemons and added water. Now, it was time to taste it. Charli frowned and squinted her eyes. Her sweet drink was as sour as could be. She forgot to add the sugar.

Charli stirred and stirred the sugar tasting it to see if it was as sweet as she wanted.

"Mom, what else makes lemonade sweet?" Charli asked.

"Honey," Mom said.

So, Charli added some honey and ice and... *Voilà!*... Charli's secret ingredient, honey, made the perfect lemonade.

The next day, Charli's mom was hosting a girlfriend's brunch at their house and Charli had another big idea, "I will serve my delicious lemonade to my mom's friends."

Charli heard all the ladies arriving. She ran to her room and put on her fancy skirt, cute long socks, pretty blouse, and pearls.

She wanted to make a good impression and look professional, so she put on her mom's blazer and high heel shoes too.

Charli overheard one of the ladies ask for something cold to drink, so she eagerly ran downstairs to the kitchen and poured glasses of lemonade for each guest. She placed them on a tray and jumping in excitement announced, "Have no fear; Charli's homemade lemonade is here!"

All the women smiled as Charli said, "Please try my fresh squeezed lemonade... with my secret ingredient."

Amazing! Superb! Excellent! Charli heard only words of enjoyment from each of her mom's friends. And to Charli's surprise, one of the women gave her a dollar and said, "Charli, this lemonade is so good, how much for another glass?"

"Oh, yes, I would like some more," said another lady.

"Me too," someone else said.

Charli was super excited! Her face was beaming with joy as she started making more lemonade for the brunch. More lemonade meant more money from each of the ladies. Her famous honey lemonade was a hit!

INGREDIENTS

1 cup of freshly squeezed lemon juice
about 4 lemons
1 cup of sugar
1/2 cup of honey
1 cup of water

INSTRUCTIONS

Place all ingredients in a
blender. Mix for 1 minute.
Drink immediately, or
store in the fridge until
ready to serve.

Later that night, Charli went to her parents' bedroom and showed them all the money she made at the brunch.

"Mommy and Daddy," Charli said with confidence, "I have decided to start my own lemonade stand. I can use the money I make to purchase a brand-new bike."

Charli's parents were so happy to see her enthusiasm. They agreed to help her start her very own lemonade stand business.

The next week was full steam ahead. Charli and her mom shopped for glasses, straws, and other supplies on the Internet. They also went to the grocery store to get the ingredients she needed to make her lemonade. While Charli and her mom were shopping, her dad was busy building her lemonade stand.

Charli had everything she needed. Her grocery list was complete and like a true CEO, she kept all her receipts in her backpack so she would know exactly how much she spent to start her business.

The Big Day was almost here. So, Charli started making her lemonade. She set her timer to see exactly how long it would take to make a gallon of lemonade.

"Wow, Mom," she said. "It takes forty-five minutes to make three gallons of lemonade; that's a lot of work."

Then Charli checked to see how much money she had spent on supplies and how much time it took to make her lemonade. That's how she and her parents came up with a price for each cup of her ice-cold, fresh squeezed lemonade with the secret ingredient.

Charli was ready to make the big bucks. She invited all her neighbors, family, and friends to her grand opening. A line of eager supporters was there to try Charli's Honey Lemonade. It was a success.

Everyone was excited about Charli's big business adventure as a young CEO.

Charli's dad and mom said, "We are so proud of you, Charli!" They gave her big hugs and lots of kisses!

Charli bought herself a brand-new bike! She learned that with a great idea and hard work you can accomplish your goals!

About the Authors

Charli Southall is a creative and thriving young artist. She is a straight A student at Renaissance Performing Arts High School in Long Beach, California. Charli loves helping others. She volunteers at the K9 Connection working with service dogs and for the Pico branch library summer reading program. Enrolled in Chamber Honors Chorus Club, Charli loves singing and acting.

DeAnna Lewis and her husband Clint are the owners of five Wingstop and four Fatburger franchises and authors of *Faith, Family and Franchise*. Married for 24 years, they have raised three amazing children: Clinton, Jr. and Cydni, as well as their niece, Charli. DeAnna founded Boss Sisters Connect where empowerment cultivates bosses. She is also the co-founder of Girls Win Inc., a non-profit organization that helps girls ages 12-18 years old in the foster care system. DeAnna has 20 years of experience as a social worker, a Bachelor of Science degree in Business Management, and a master's degree in Educational Counseling. Passionate about giving back, DeAnna and Clint are actively involved in their church and community. They sponsor several local high schools as well as scholarships for Cal State University of Bakersfield and Harvest Connection Bakersfield and provide complete meals for over 250 families.

CONNECT WITH US at FaithFamilyFranchise.com

CPSIA information can be obtained
at www.ICGtesting.com
Printed in the USA
BVHW021551310721
613263BV00021B/1461